# Good Mourning Sunshine!

*Wake up your heart –Stop surviving and start living.*

## Angela Q. Bertone

**Ask Angela Productions**

Edited by Rachel Kovach.
Book cover design by Lucia Young.

ISBN-13:
978-0615577395

ISBN-10:
0615577393

*Library of Congress cataloging registration:*
*Bertone, Angela Q.*
*Good Mourning Sunshine*

# Dedication

This book was written at the request of my friends who allowed me the honor of teaching them through the years.

Thank you to everyone who assisted me and sacrificed time to help me complete this work. Especially to my dear friend, Kim Kern, who allowed me to call her anytime, day or night, to beacon her help.

I dedicate this book to my Mom, Sarah Lou Quezada, who gave me the gift of story telling, writing, imagination and most of all, *her love*. She introduced me to the study of words during a challenging time in my life . . . an introduction, which would forever alter my way of thinking, studying, teaching and living.

Thank you Mom, for believing in me and taking the time to share with me your love of words. In your passing I have entered into another chapter of life. Inside this arena of sorrow I am comforted by the things you taught me, which shower my heart and soul everyday.

# Preface

I would like to take a moment to prepare you for what I hope will be a life changing experience for you. This book is an expression of my heart and depicts a very remarkable time in my life. In an attempt to bring you into my private encounters with God, you're invited to eavesdrop on my unusual discussions with him. You will see my frustrations and share in my shock and judgments of God as he spoke to me in ways I never considered he would.

There were times when I felt he was ripping me apart or shaking my very foundation; on occasion it was difficult to feel his love. Yet, in the gentleness of his spirit, he gave me understanding as to what he was showing me.

Listening without feeling defensive was difficult. I discovered how quickly I judged God. As if he did not know how to speak to me the way I needed. I learned he uses whatever I need to get my attention.

I caution you to keep an open mind to the fact this book is based on my own perception. I am simply being as open as I can be, bearing my very soul, and pouring out the insight I gained and felt during this journey.

In addition, I worked very hard to keep the experience as true as possible, by working from my memory, my poetry and my study notes. It was suggested by some to take out the conversations I had with God and to simply teach you what I had learned. I struggled with whether or not to change my writings, and ultimately came to the conclusion that if I did; I was somehow taking credit for the amazing wisdom being given to me. In doing so I would be presumptuous to portray myself as the teacher, when in fact I was and remain to be . . . the student.

# *Prologue*

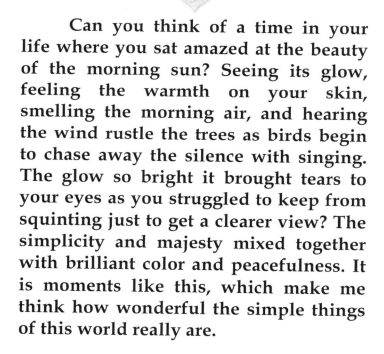

Can you think of a time in your life where you sat amazed at the beauty of the morning sun? Seeing its glow, feeling the warmth on your skin, smelling the morning air, and hearing the wind rustle the trees as birds begin to chase away the silence with singing. The glow so bright it brought tears to your eyes as you struggled to keep from squinting just to get a clearer view? The simplicity and majesty mixed together with brilliant color and peacefulness. It is moments like this, which make me think how wonderful the simple things of this world really are.

I have experienced a sunrise many different times, and it seems all of them are somehow just as amazing. I never grow weary of the experience. When I am there in the midst of the moment, I wonder why I do not get up everyday just to relive the joy again and again.

A man named Paul spoke of a mystery where all creation, including the sunrise is actually speaking to us? Even with all of my senses engaged in the experience, I had never heard the sun actually speak to me of some great life mystery. I honestly had no clue as to the reality of what Paul spoke until it happened to me. "A talking creation?"

Have you ever lost a loved one to death? Isn't it true in the separation from this person, you woke up to the depth of how much you truly love that person? Did you ever hear the sunrise speak of this truth?

You may agree with it, because The Truth is already in you. But the question is have you ever *heard* the Sun speak of this truth?

My guess is that like me, you too had never heard the sun speak. Paul taught about a language spoken by creation, but another man named Isaiah prophesied we would all be blind and deaf. Perhaps, this is the reason why I could not hear the universe actually speak. I never considered this language or attempted to understand it until I had an unbelievable experience. Besides, who am I that the universe would acknowledge or speak to me?

Many years ago some religious leaders questioned Jesus and argued, "we are not blind."

Jesus responded, *"If you had just said you were blind, none of this would be held against you, but because you say, you can see, all this shall be held against you."*

John 9:41

Again, I did not think this blindness included me. I thought it meant those religious people, and somehow I was different.

Buddhists speak of enlightenment as a journey, as though it is commonly understood we are in some kind of darkness. Other religions as well speak of some type of blindness, as though it is a universal truth. Yet, I thought I was somehow exempt.

I was taught when I asked God to forgive me of my sin, and I gave my heart to Him, I was no longer blind. Like the well-known words of Amazing Grace, "I once was blind, but now I see." I thought God had enlightened my eyes because I had become a Christian. I couldn't have been more wrong.

After this amazing experience, when I heard the universe (creation) speak to me, I began to realize my eyes are in a state of blindness. I am discovering I only see in part. Therefore, my understanding is also partial, skewed, or in other words twisted. The words twisted and wicked are one in the same. Wicked comes from the Latin term "wicker" which, like a wicker basket, literally means to twist and craft.

Because everyone has their own perception of life from their current position in life, and because each perception is molded by our past experiences, our view is not complete. It is only one view, a one-sided perception. However, God's view is perfect. So if we rely on our own perception it will always be slighted, impaired, twisted, or wicked. What would life be like if we could only see through God's perception?

Paul taught all life's mysteries are *clearly* seen in creation including God and all His power. Again I ask you, have you ever heard creation talk to you? Has creation clearly shown you all of life's mysteries? Has anyone ever taught you about this creation language? Can you hear and understand it?

Are you convinced our perception is off, and we are all blind? I would like to share with you some of my "ah-ha" moments as I began to hear the universe speak, and I began to realize just how blind I truly am.

# Chapter 1
## The Beauty of the Morning.

Early one morning while driving to work, as I watched the warm orange sunrise, I heard a voice say, *"In the morning you wake up."*

I responded candidly, "I know."

*"No,"* the voice persisted, *"listen again. In the MOURNING you wake up."*

Fear struck my heart, my palms began to sweat, and I could hear my heart beat in my ears.

"Oh, God! Is something bad about to happen to my children? My husband? My family? What are you telling me?"

The voice responded, *"I am simply teaching you, not warning you."*

"Do you know how much you love your children?"

"Yes," I replied.

"No you don't. Not unless I took them from you, could you understand how much you love them. You see, in the _mourning_ you wake up."

"Lord, why are you telling me this? Are you preparing me for something bad?"

Again, "No," was the reply.

"Understand. When you suffer, grieve, mourn, and are broken, you enter into a different level of awareness and understanding. You wake up. You are able to see. You acquire understanding.

*The sunrise has been telling you of this truth, your whole life, but you have been blind and deaf, unable to perceive it. I am just allowing you to see and hear with my eyes and ears, so that you can hear and see the truth."*

As you can imagine, tears were streaming down my face. I continued driving on to work, crying and confused. As I sat in amazement I thought to myself; I can never tell anyone this story, they will think I have lost my mind.

When I went inside my office, the women I worked with asked what happened to me. "Why," I asked? They told me I looked sun burned. I ran to the bathroom to see. I was beat red, my face, my chest, all over. This was a very surreal experience. The thought of God himself teaching me almost made me feel crazy. However, the truth of what I heard was undeniable. *"In the mourning you wake up."* How true this really is.

If I had never heard the creation speak truth before this experience, how much more truth is out there for me to see and hear? This thought overwhelmed me, as I looked at my red face and neck in the bathroom mirror, tears still streaming down my face.

My relationship with God would never be the same. Over a short period of time I began to hear Him like never before. It was becoming easier and easier to know the difference between my own thoughts and God's voice. The way He talked to me was unbelievable. His words were so contrary to my belief and way of thinking. The voice was clearly not that of my own words or of my own thoughts. I actually found myself arguing with God about truth. As if I knew what I was talking about. "But your Word says..." had become my biggest argument.

My prayer life had actually morphed into conversation. God was teaching me I only knew what I had been taught by other people about His word. Now, God was teaching me. What was happening to me? Who would ever believe this if I dare tell anyone?

Over the next few weeks it was difficult to accomplish even daily tasks. I struggled to get the kids to school or clean my home, much less go to work. All I wanted to do was read and talk to God. The conversations continued often until 2 a.m. Sometimes I would ask God to just let me rest and please stop my thoughts. I wondered if I was possibly having a nervous breakdown. This seemed uncalled for because my life was so wonderful and my heart seemed at peace.

I dare not tell the whole story because why should anyone believe me. There was no apparent reason for me to be going through this experience. The undeniable truth of God's voice kept me relentlessly seeking him. This wisdom could not come from any person; it had to be from God.

*"I am teaching you, the whole earth has been speaking of me since the beginning of time, just as Paul taught. If you believe in the prophets and understand, you would know Isaiah was sent to make mankind blind and deaf. He was grieved over this request and beckoned me, 'how long, Oh Lord?' The response was, 'Until they are destroyed.'"*

"But this seems mean. Why would you want to destroy your people if you love them?"

"I do not desire destruction. I desire relationship. You assume destruction is bad. I am not afraid of destruction, because I understand it is a beginning not an end. Since creation, mankind has attempted to make decisions and live out of their own strength apart from me. Humans have decided to live by what they deem to be good or evil. However the consequence of this desire is death or better spoken 'separation from me.'

I am not afraid of your discovery of living apart from relationship with me. I know what you call failures are actually life's lessons, which will cause you to grow and mature. The nature of life will actually bring you back into relationship with me, and the latter shall be greater than the former. Life without relationship is actually death or separation. This separation from me will cause you to desire life with relationship once again. Your so-called failure is a gift, which will open your eyes, in time, and like a seed produce much fruit.

*Children often think they know better than their parents, sometimes they actually must walk through life experiences before they believe what their parents have told them. They do this because they lack the knowledge and wisdom gained in living. Ignoring a parent's correction is part of the natural curiosity of humans. It is neither good nor bad.*

*Discovery through pain and sorrow oftentimes is the only road to the truth. Truth is Me, and I Am Truth. Therefore you are actually returning to relationship even in your separation.*

*When pain confirms the parent's warnings trust is established. Either relationship with the parent, or rules to live by, becomes the foundation for the child's life. Currently, most people attempt to know me by rules. In time, they will discover rules do not produce relationship; they actually destroy it.*

*I desire relationship, not rules of right and wrong. Destruction is not always as it appears. For example, a seed is destroyed in the mystery of planting and reaping. But the destruction is not the end of the seed; rather it is a new beginning of life, a cycle.*

*Humans are on a journey of being free to fall and even destroy their selves to bring into existence true oneness with God and man. I am not punishing my children so they will obey me. Rather, I am letting them discover who they are and who they are not. I am not afraid of destruction, because I understand the nature of life and death. You see it as an end. I see it for what it is.*

*When the time is full and humanity has discovered the truth that is already in them, mankind will awaken and life will take on a new dimension."*

"I do not understand what you are talking about."

*"That is okay, in time you shall. For now, let's just focus on our relationship and knowing each other. You must first get to know yourself, before you can know others; including Me.*

*You will not like yourself at first. This will take some time. You have spent most of your life trying to be what you have defined as a good person. However, you are only human. Good and bad are relative. That is why you can never attain 'goodness.'*

*When you begin to see yourself as you are, it will be difficult. However, I will be with you and you will learn what love is and what love is not. You will discover I love you no matter what you do or have ever done. I love YOU, not what you do or don't do.*

# *Journal*

# Chapter 2

## Our 5 Senses.

Sight, smell, taste, touch and hearing. These are things of the physical creation, which teach us about the spiritual person inside of us all.

With our physical senses we experience and perceive the world around us. We even learn how to speak and have relationship through them.

Helen Keller was blind and deaf, but miraculously learned to speak without these two of her senses. She used taste, touch and feeling to experience and perceive the world. She was forced to learn how to communicate and have relationship without sight or sound. How amazing is that?

Can you imagine having to learn about your world this way? Well, if we believe we are spiritually blind and deaf, we too must use our other senses to learn to speak and have relationship spiritually.

Many people have questioned me about talking to God. "Do you actually hear Him?" they ask. This makes me think they must not. I tell them I did not always hear God like I do now and currently there are times I am not able to hear like I want. Often times, I feel deaf when I pray.

I have learned how to use my other senses to hear God, mainly my sense of touch. To touch is the same as to feel. The spiritual way to feel is through your emotions. However, at first my emotions were so sick and underdeveloped they were not reliable. I had spent my life trying to feel good and to escape all feelings of pain.

Therefore, my emotions were tangled and crippled. It took me years of allowing myself to feel, and submitting my feelings to prayer, before I could began to understand how precious they actually are.

Like Helen, I needed my feelings to hear. To hear whom you might ask? God. I wanted to hear God and he spoke to me in my heart. The problem was my head usually got in the way and twisted the message God was delivering through my emotions. I came to understand emotions are neither good nor bad. They just are. I began to depend on God to help me through the feelings and not escape them. My emotions became my life-line to God. I must admit, I was often confused but in time I began to understand the language and I will share some of these truths with you.

I hope it will help you to open your heart and start on a new journey with God as your personal teacher. Many people do not understand how a painful emotion can be useful to me and why I would want to listen. My response is that it usually reveals some lie I have embraced as truth.

For example, if someone I care about rejects me, I feel emotional pain. This is a normal response. However, another person's rejection does not place me in a constant state of rejection. I have learned to seek to understand the other person's heart and feelings to try and see what they may have been going through. It is kind of like a cup. You can only pour out of a cup what someone has put into the cup. So I guess you can say my pain makes me look at others differently.

It also reminds me I may still be harboring fear. Like the fear of being rejected. If I love myself and know God loves me, then I can go through the feelings of rejection and know I am not in a state of rejection. Feelings alone are not the truth. It is the language. God speaks to me through my feelings, all of them. When I have pain and I remember to ask God about it, he answers me. He reveals the meaning behind my feelings.

If I rely on my life's experiences to teach me, or bring back a lesson of the past, then I miss out on the opportunity to learn from God in the present. Most of the time pain from the past causes me to look to myself for the answer. I usually respond in some defensive way and then remember to go to God. I wish I could say I always go to God first, but you know that would be a lie. I am getting better at it though. It is like falling down. You get tired of the bumps and bruises and you learn how to walk. However, just because you can walk doesn't mean you will never fall again.

Pain wakes us up. Attempting to escape causes our senses to be desensitized. I hope by giving you some of my experiences with pain you will see all of your emotions are a gift to help you. Go through the pain and look into your heart to find truth in the midst of your pain and sorrow. No farmer plants a seed expecting it to do nothing. He plants it expecting a reward. I have found in my life when I go through my sorrows and suffering with God as my teacher, my life always changes for the better; and when I try to escape my pain, it only causes more problems.

If you are blind and deaf like me then you will need to rely on your touch, smell and taste. So let's see if I can help to explain how this has worked for me.

All of our senses have one thing in common. They give us understanding. They guide us, teach us and help us to experience the physical. Our heart (Spirit) does the same thing through emotions. We experience relationship through our emotions. If we are unable to connect on an emotional level there is no relationship. Relationships need to experience understanding, acceptance, love, compassion, kindness, caring, connection, passion . . . All of which are achieved in the emotions.

Our brain on the other hand does the thinking about the emotions. This is where most of our problems lie. Our brain has memory and our emotions are connected to memory as well as our five senses.

God has taught me to rely on Him for the explanation of the feelings and not to rely on my memory alone. To rely on my memory causes me to seek control to avoid pain. To avoid pain is an illusion. With life and relationship, comes pain. Relying on God is about trusting even when I do go through pain, He is there with me.

I am not suggesting we go through life ignoring cause and effect. I realize if I touch the fire, it will burn. I am talking about relying on God to explain why I am feeling a particular feeling, instead of relying on my own understanding of what I interpret my feelings to mean.

Initially, when I feel a painful emotion, I unconsciously go through my memory bank looking for an explanation as to how or why I feel a certain way. I am going to name this process "Pink." I know this sounds a little weird, but bear with me.

I am going to call seeking God for the answers to what I am feeling and why, "Red and White."

As a child we learn our colors and accept they are what our teacher tells us. Red, blue, green, yellow, orange, purple, white, brown, black, pink . . .

Then a little later in life someone introduces us to paint. In the process of painting we discover when you mix colors together they take on a new color and the shades are endless.

Emotions are the same. When we are little, someone sees us crying and says, "What is wrong?"

Unconsciously we perceive crying as wrong. Our life teachers have defined for us anger, fear, sadness, joy, happiness, etc. We accumulate a bank of memories over a lifetime we learn to rely on to explain our current emotional condition; "Pink."

Then God comes along and says what you perceive as "pink" in your current bank of information, is also "red and white." (A different way to interpret the same feelings). Red and white can come in endless forms and shades. The reasons for your feelings are endless too. We are simply quick to put a label on the feeling instead of relying on God to give us the understanding.

Now we have a dilemma. We know pink, we have known pink all of our lives, and now someone comes along and says no, this is red and white. If we have not experienced paint and seen red and white being mixed together, it would be impossible to believe. However, if we were given the opportunity to actually mix the paint and watch it transform into pink, it would be possible to believe.

Understanding our emotions is just like this. When I began to ask God to teach me about my emotions, it started a lifetime of lessons, which I have come to accept will continue forever. I would like to let you know, just because I understand this concept and teach others, I am by no means an expert at walking it out. When I experience painful emotions, the first thing I see is still pink. Shortly thereafter, I am reminded they are actually red and white. Let me help you with a story or two.

During this time in my life God liked to get my attention while I was driving. I guess it was one of the few times in my life I was quiet. Anyway, I was driving home and I got this sick feeling in my stomach. It was the feeling I commonly associated with women's intuition, which tells me something is wrong. (PINK). "Oh God, what is the matter," was my gut response.

*"Nothing is the matter. Does something need to be wrong for me to make my presence known?"*

"No, but if nothing is wrong, why does this feels so bad. It hurts. My stomach feels like it is in knots and turning."

*"I am all power and power can hurt. Would it feel good if you put a 110 volt wire in our stomach?"*

"Of course not, it would be very painful."

*"Exactly, and I am All Powerful. You prayed saying you wanted to feel more of me, and I am tempering your spirit to handle more power; More of my presence."* (Red & White)

I accepted what he was telling me, and the rest of the way home I just let this unpleasant feeling flow through me without resistance, worry or fear. Peace like I had never known or felt poured over me like thick oil.

In times past, I would have been praying in fear for all of my loved ones begging God to protect them. This is kind of weird, because if we do anything without faith, it is impossible to please God. Up to this point, I prayed in fear not even realizing my lack of faith.

I asked God to help me teach this to others and he gave me another example. Let's pretend we could put our feelings into a bucket, and I had three different feelings. Let's also assume all three of them were small course granules. The first is sand, the second is salt and the third is sugar. Let's assume you are deaf and blind and I set all three buckets in front of you and I guide your hand into one of the buckets. Your first instinct might be, "Oh, this is salt." Then, I guide your hand into the second bucket, but it feels just the same, and the third also feels the same. Based on your past memories, you search for what they could be.

You consider all three, sand, salt, and sugar. You also consider borax, minerals or some unknown poison. You realize you could use your smell or taste to give you a better understanding, but what if it was poison. It would be best if you relied on your teacher to tell you rather than relying on your other two senses. You may go so far as to smell, but you may not want to taste it just in case it was harmful.

Our first instinct is to observe where we are and what we are experiencing and then label our feelings. Just like me on my way home, when I assumed something was wrong, because I thought I knew what the feelings in my heart meant. Just like assuming the bucket was filled with salt. We often rush to judgment of our emotions, (Pink), instead of asking our teacher, "What is this feeling, Lord, what are you showing me?" (Red & White).

Training my mind to work like this, sure took a long time. Even now, I see pink first. However, almost instantly I am reminded, oh yeah, this is really Red and White. Yielding our thoughts to the God of all creation takes time, just remember, we are human and it is our nature to rely on our own way of thinking. The good news is that this makes it easier to hear God, because our thoughts are so different from his.

I find it an interesting fact we acquire wax in our ears. A wax build up can actually impair our hearing. Consider this; wax is bitter. Have your ever held bitter feelings in your heart against someone, and then find it hard to consider their point of view? You can't hear or accept their perspective without forgiveness.

Hands develop calluses after being subjected to the pain of a hammer. Your unconscious self feels the pain of the hammer, and sends messages to the hand to hold on to that dead skin; we will need it later for protection.

We do the same thing emotionally when someone hurts our feeling. Oh, we say we forgive them, but we don't forget (hold on to that dead stuff). Sounds like a callus to me.

Our nose can also become callused. Have you ever heard the saying, "Pig farmers don't smell pig poop." We do the same thing for many different reasons.

I have a friend who was angry all the time at her daughter. She had no idea she even felt that way, much less why. She was immune to her own feelings for her own child. One day, I asked her what was wrong. After she said nothing, I asked permission to describe what I witnessed in their presence and she very humbly asked for me to share my observation.

She and I were in a room filled with family and friends and no one was angry. Then her daughter walked into the room and her whole countenance changed. Her body became stiff and ridged, her face changed to a hard glare, and the way she spoke became sharp and insensitive. This was totally out of her character and I had never seen her this way. When I told her this she could not believe it. Because she trusted me, she took what I said and asked God to help her see.

The very next time she and her daughter were together, her anger immediately became apparent, but she had no clue as to why. This began a journey between her and God, which I will not share at this time. My friend's story shows us how we can become callused, because even though anger was all around her and all over her, like the pig farmer; she could not even smell it.

Relating our emotions to our five senses is a very difficult concept to grasp. I am still learning new things through this part of creation and I hope my understanding in this area continues to expand until the day I die. Do not be discouraged if you feel some confusion. Hang in there and ask God to help you. He is faithful, and all of his creation is here to assist us.

# *Journal*

_____

_____

_____

_____

_____

_____

_____

_____

_____

_____

_____

_____

# *Chapter 3*
## *All Life Comes Through Brokenness.*

"Mourning wakes me up." I did not like this truth. Why does it have to be this way? This seems so mean and cruel. How can a loving God make life this way? Surely He could have come up with something else.

When I asked God about this process He told me, *"You ask for faith, and doubt is given, for only in doubt is faith seen. You ask for hope and despair comes, for only in despair can hope be revealed. You ask for mercy and offenses come, for only then is mercy given, and you ask for love and death is given, for only in death can the depth of love be revealed. To 'know' is painful, but worth it.*

*Curiosity is in your very nature. Knowing cannot be taught by words alone. Experience teaches you what words cannot. In time you will desire relationship more than knowledge. There is a time for everything.*

*Have you ever considered a seed?*

*The gardener must <u>break</u> open the dirt before he can put the seed into the ground. Where then, it is surrounded by darkness. The seed must be <u>broken</u> by the heat of the sun and the swelling of the moisture. Then the roots go deeper into the darkness of the soil, after which the plant <u>breaks</u> the ground yet again to reach the open air above the earth. Then after the plant puts forth a bud, the bud must <u>break</u> open, so that the flower can bloom. The flower <u>dies</u> to make way for the fruit. The fruit is <u>sacrificed</u> for the gardener to eat. The fruit is produced for the life of the gardener.*

*It is as simple as a cycle of dying to live and living to die. Does the gardener consider this as cruel to the life contained within the seed?"*

God showed me this is what happens to me when I hear God and then I try to obey Him. His word is the seed. My heart is the dirt. My brain lacks understanding and I feel like I am in the dark, and confused. My attempt to obey Him fails (the seed dies). Sometimes it takes me longer than others to realize I cannot keep all of the rules. My heart cries, and my chest swells with sorrow when I feel like I have failed God. I sometimes feel as if I am further away from Him as I go deeper into depression or confusion. Then somehow, from somewhere, like the mystery of photosynthesis, life springs out of me. God opens my heart and with understanding shows me He is the life of His Word.

His Word is the Seed, and I must be broken, until his Word produces life within me. Seeds are not put into my heart to be performed, but they are put in my heart to die, so God can bring forth His Word in my life. Every time I experience this, I feel rejuvenated and ready to face the world yet again. The fruit in my life is never of me. It is God bringing life out of me when I cannot. It became clear to me that carved fruit made from wax, glass, wood, or in other words, from my own efforts at obedience, are not edible. I desire the fruit derived from his Seed.

When a baby is conceived the hymen must be _broken_ for the male to plant the seed in the woman. The sperm _breaks_ through the egg and the two become one. The baby grows and is one with the mother. Then in _labor,_ the water must _break,_ and produce the birth of life. And yet again the umbilical cord must be _cut_ and the child and mother who are living by one blood supply must end, so that the child can live.

The word hymen is the same word used on our church song books we call hymnals. It means to be broken. When the man breaks the hymen, it bleeds and is painful. Then in rhythm, the seed is deposited in the womb, (a place from which life comes). Then in secret (darkness) the seed grows and life comes forth. God's word is the seed, our hearts, in a state of brokenness is like the womb, bloody and ready to receive. Yet, how and when life will return or come forth is a mystery. But just like a baby, it will be laborious, painful, and concealed in darkness or mystery. When the birth happens it is a gift, not a work of our own hands, or a decision of our will.

A carpenter must cut down the tree, dry the wood and then cut the tree yet again and again. By doing this he can build a home or a piece of furniture. But without the cutting process he can only imagine it.

Life will sometimes cut us down, leave us dry and dead on the inside. It can appear we are no longer good for anything. But this cutting process, builds character, integrity, compassion and other qualities. These attributes are constructed over time and are not easily acquired.

A glassmaker must destroy the sand by heat in order to produce glass. Everything we eat has to die for us to live. In order to be heard, we must break the silence. In music, a record is cut. Diamonds are cut into pieces of jewelry. Gold and silver are melted down. In learning to walk we all fall down. To build his own family, a man must first leave his mother and father. When the warmth of a fire is needed something must be burned. The gardener grows the grapes in order to crush and transform their juice into wine. An atom needs both a positive and negative electric charge to exist. Without rain there is no rainbow.

Everything is made to be broken. But the suffering is not worthy to be compared to the joy that is to come. When we consider these truths do we think this is mean and cruel?

Life without brokenness and pain is only an illusion. Life comes through this process. Look at nature: hear, see, and understand. Pain is something most of us have spent our lives escaping, or at least attempting to. However, pain itself is one of life's gifts, which yields understanding and character.

Without pain, we would not realize fire could consume us if we continued touching it. When a child is told the fire is hot he repeats you and says, "hot, huh Mama?" But he does not actually understand it until he feels the pain. The pain causes the child to connect the word 'hot' to the suffering he has just felt. Only now does he know it is hot.

Yet, if you tell the same child a pepper is hot and he touches it, and feels no pain; he will argue and persist to tell you, "look Mama, it's not hot, see, you can touch it." He cannot realize there is more than one dimension of hot. Not until he tastes it will he understand it is hot . . . a different kind of hot.

Even after acquiring the knowledge and understanding of what hot means, he can still lack understanding. For example, if a child burns his finger and gets a blister, he definitely has a deeper level of understanding, but he cannot imagine the pain of a person who has been burned all over his body. His mind can only attempt to imagine. The only way to fully comprehend this type of pain would be for him to actually have the same degree of burns. This type of understanding is the same word as to "know". Through this experience, the child's feelings and emotions give way to understanding, and he can truly "know" the pain.

This truth carries over into emotional pain as well. If I have never lost a child, it is impossible for me to fully understand this type of grief. I can attempt to imagine the pain, and even feel fear, sorrow, dread, grief and despair. I may even feel sick to my stomach or depressed. However, it is impossible for me to actually feel the full degree of that person's suffering without the loss of a child. This is an understanding I never want to endure.

I have interviewed numerous parents who have lost a child and discussed this truth. All of them have confirmed this to be so. One of the worst things we can tell another person who is suffering this kind of loss is "we understand" if we have never lost in this way. "NO, YOU DON'T" is their intense inner reply. Most parents just suffer in silence, because they understand we are trying to comfort them. It is just better to say nothing than to make such an insensitive hurtful statement.

I do not attempt to convey loss and suffering as things we should welcome by any means. I am simply saying life will bring pain whether or not we are ready. By realizing, accepting and understanding it is the way of life, maybe we can go through our sorrows and still find life on the other side. Furthermore, when we do find life on the other side, it does not mean sorrow will not return, for it is part of the cycle of living.

Broken... Hearts, seeds, wombs, skin, dreams, lives, families - all brokenness brings forth new life.

We have been trained to be afraid of pain and to avoid it at all cost. It is our human nature. However, avoiding pain is not actually possible. Our attempts are futile. So what can we do? We can understand the need for pain, and learn healthy skills for healthy relationships; first with ourselves and God, and then relationship with others.

Accepting pain, mourning, suffering, tears, and grief are continually present in my life, which can at times be depressing and overwhelming. But realizing they cannot be avoided is the first step to living. Attempting to escape is a never-ending _battle,_ not a life.

Finding the silver lining in life is one way to accept pain. Suffering can bring about change and understanding. I am learning different ways to go through the pain and not to run from it. Trusting in this new knowledge and accepting emotional pain does not destroy you, although it is difficult. Take some time to consider how running from pain has caused detriment in your life.

Can you see in your life where you have used any of the following to escape your emotional suffering?

Food, alcohol, sex, work, religion, anger, depression, victimization, isolation, revenge, hatred, money, self-righteousness, jealousy, materialism, pride, justification, blame, minimization, rationalization, manipulation, control, avoidance, silence, excessive-talking, disconnect, criticism, etc . . .

*In the mourning you wake up.*

To us it only seems right to escape the pain life brings our way. However, escaping it is only an illusion. There is no such thing. Suffering is a part of life that can bring about great change. Trying to escape is a fruitless lie.

I heard when an eagle is overtaken by a storm he must fly headfirst into the wind and rain. By doing so the wind under his wings will lift him up above the storm, providing a new perception from above. If he tries to out fly the storm he is at risk of being overtaken by it. The same is true for us. If we try to run from pain we only make it worse. By facing our storms we acquire a new perception. When we face our sorrows, and feel our feelings, we acquire understanding.

Even so, true understanding can be delayed in the midst of pain, and for me usually arrives later in a time of reflection. However, if I don't focus on escaping, and I focus on letting the feelings pass through my body; I gain understanding and learn to truly live.

So, what does it mean to let the feelings pass through your body? Exactly that. I may be sitting or lying down. I try to clear my mind of any thought process and just relax into the pain. I do not try to make it go away. I simply let the pain flow kind of like water through my entire body. At some point the pain actually subsides. My prayer through this kind of experience may be something like . . .

"Lord, I do not understand why I must go through this, but I know you live in me and you are understanding. I trust you are my strength, and the life that is in me is actually you. Therefore, these feelings are you and your power at work in my life. I don't know what you are doing or why, but I trust you. Do with me as you will."

Then, I do nothing. If I cry, so be it. If I need to scream or just sit in silence, I do simply that. Basically there are no rules. I just let my feelings be whatever they are, until they pass. Like a ripened fruit on the vine, understanding takes time to mature. God decides when I am ready for His understanding.

# Journal

# *Chapter 4*

## *Without Darkness, You Cannot See.*

*"Without darkness you cannot see."*

**"No Lord, without light, I cannot see."**

*"What if I put two lights in your eyes like at the doctor's office? What could you see?"*

**"Nothing."**

*"Exactly! Nothing; you would be blinded for the moment. When light and darkness are both present, you are able to see. However, you have decided you do not like darkness. You have been taught darkness is bad. Darkness is not a thing; it is the absence of light. Full light makes you blind. Your eyes need a measure of light to see. Too much light will cause you to be blind. Therefore, without darkness you cannot see.*

*Darkness or shadows are necessary for you to see dimension. You must learn to love the shadow side of yourself."*

"But Lord, I don't want to love that part of me. I want you to change that part of me. I want to be good."

*"When you look into the night sky what do you see?"*

I stopped and closed my eyes and imagined a beautiful starlit night, with a beautiful crescent moon against a blanket of midnight. With a deep breath and sigh I replied; "The stars."

*"Exactly. Why do you not look at the darkness? The darkness takes up much more space than the light. Without the blackness of midnight you cannot see the beauty of the stars. Where are the stars in the noon of day?"*

"They are still there."

*"Yes, but why can't you see them? Now do you understand without darkness, you cannot see?*

*Unless you learn to look at the darkness that is in you and love yourself the way you are, you will be deceived into thinking the love and kindness, which comes out of you is of your own ability. You will deceive yourself into thinking you are good.*

*However, Jesus said only my Father is good. I am love, kindness, patience, and so much more than you can imagine. When you think you have shown love, it is an illusion. Your nature is revenge, blame, hatred, and justice. My nature is mercy, love, and forgiveness. I do not give love, I am love. That is why I give you myself. That is why I live in you. I love you.*

*If you or someone else witnesses love coming out of you, it is like the stars in the night sky. I am the way, the truth, and the light. I am love. You are like the midnight sky, which allows the light of the stars to be seen. Remember the quote in the Bible that says "the Light came into the darkness and the darkness perceived it not." That was talking about the condition of man. You are that darkness. The Light which came into you was me, but you did not perceive it was me. Therefore, you have mistakenly concluded the light which comes out of you is of your own will."*

I then heard Jesus ask me, *"Do you think I am good?"*

"Yes Lord; I know you are good."

*"Really? Then you must also believe I am a liar?"*

"Oh, no Lord. I do not think you are a liar."

*"Do you not remember when a man in the Bible called Jesus good master. Jesus corrected him, and told him there was only one who was good and that was his Father?"*

"Yes, I remember."

*"Then which one is the truth. Either I am not good or I lied. You assume not good equals bad. That is not true. What is your answer? Am I not good, or am I a liar."*

I did not want to answer, because either answer I gave made me feel bad, as though I was criticizing God. However, I had to answer He was not good and He had not lied.

*"Why then do you try to be good if you know I am not? Are you trying to be better than me? Are you attempting to be my Father?"*

Wow! What a question. I was really in a dilemma now. For you see I had spent my entire life trying to be good. I decided in order for me to be loved by God, others, and even to love myself, being good was the only way. I could not answer him because there was no need to. My futile attempts to be good were evidence against me.

Let me make it clear. I believe in my heart Jesus saved me. But I convinced myself I was showing my gratitude by being a good person, even though I know I cannot earn God's love. But now that he was asking me this question, it was revealing a deeper part of my motives. Motives I did not realize existed.

God showed me not to acquire my self-worth by being a good person; rather, I should love the shadow side of me . . . the ugly part I have always tried to remedy. Learning to love my darkness is a concept I was not so sure about.

I began to realize I had deceived others and myself into thinking I was pretty good; at least most of the time. My pastor would even from time to time admonish my family and I as an example to follow. Friends and family also complimented my accomplishments.

God continued to show me darkness was necessary to see. One night, I watched a movie about two young boys who got lost in a blizzard for five days. Because of the whiteness of the snow and the lack of any other color, a condition called snow-blindness overcame the young boys. After such a long time of the pupils being exposed to the sunlight reflecting off of the glistening snow, the eyes perceived everything as black: snow-blindness.

I had never heard of this before. It was almost unbelievable, God used the movie to show me this fact, at the same time He was teaching me, *"without darkness you cannot see."* Even as I was 2000 miles away from home, on vacation watching television, God continued to teach me this lesson on understanding the need for darkness.

Another example he gave me was a blank white canvas. Look at this canvas. What do you see? Nothing. Exactly. It has no darkness. No color. Darkness is the absence of something. Darkness is not a something; it is an adjective that describes the condition of something.

Light contains all wavelengths of color and gives them all away at the same time. When an object is in the presence of light, it reflects light. The color something appears to be, is because it is the only color the object is not holding onto. So if you see a red ball, it is not actually red. It is absorbing all the colors except red. It reflects the red and your eyes perceive it as red. The object is actually every color except red. It is absent of red light waves. It is the absence of something that gives you perception.

Dimension is a form of understanding. Without it we cannot see. Darkness is necessary. Because of our perception of darkness, we think it is bad. However, darkness is not the culprit; it is our perception that is twisted.

# Journal

_____

_____

_____

_____

_____

_____

_____

_____

_____

_____

_____

# Chapter 5
## Thank You God I Am Not Like Her.

One day while washing dishes in my new home, I began to thank God for all of my blessings. My gratitude was genuine and heartfelt. I was grateful for the usual things: my children, my husband, our relationship, our health, our new home and our financial state . . . all of God's blessings.

I was remembering the news show I watched the night before about a prostitute who was interviewed by a famous female news anchor. The prostitute was an addict and refused the news anchor's offer to help change her life.

The prostitute showed her badly tract-scarred arms and said, "Look at me. I can never change. I am an addict. Who would ever want me? Who would trust me? Do you know how many times I have tried to change? Thank you, but I have always been and will always be a whore."

As you can image I was shocked at her refusal for help.

As I thanked God for my blessings, I began to thank God I was not an addict and I was not like the lady who did not believe she could be helped. I felt so sorry for her and began to pray and cry for her. I was overwhelmingly sad.

Then I heard: *"The tax collector is justified, but you are not."*

"Oh God! I love you and I have prayed and accepted Jesus as my Savior. I am born again. What do you mean I am not justified?" Silence.

*"To whom much is forgiven loveth much. You have not done much. You have just thanked me that you have not. You are thankful for your life of goodness."*

"Yes, I know, but I love you with all I have."

*"I know; it is just not very much."*

"I am confused. What do you want me to do, go out and sin more so I can love you more?"

*"No,"* was his reply. *"You have already done enough; you are just blind to your ways. You are already everything you have judged. Just like the woman in the TV show last night. You just don't know it."*

"What do you mean God? I have never known any man except my husband, and I have never even tried drugs."

*"I know, but how long shall you doubt? You adulterous generation."*

**"What are you saying? How is doubt and adultery the same?"**

*"Who is the Father of all lies?"*

**"Satan."**

*"Only lies produce doubt. So who have you been intimate with?"*

**"Wait. Are you telling me believing a lie is being intimate with Satan?"**

*"Do you not understand words are seeds? A Father must be intimate to plant his seed. If Satan is the Father of lies, how else can you conceive a lie?*

*Now do you see you are already like the whore on the TV show? You are a spiritual whore. You judged her and you are no different.*

You have said in your heart if a husband commits adultery against his wife, this means he does not really love her, correct?"

"Yes Lord. I have said this."

"Then it must also be true you cannot really love me, if you commit adultery with Satan."

"Oh, God! Have mercy on me. I did not realize. I did not know. I am a human. Is it possible for me to never doubt again."

"So you do understand how the harlot believed she could never be anything else except a harlot. Are you not addicted to lies and doubting?

Do you believe with me all things are possible?"

"I have said so and I think I believe. However, I am so confused. I am realizing I do not even know myself, or my condition. I am so ashamed. Please God, help me!"

I lay on my hardwood floor, in a fetal position crying for what seemed like forever. I cried until there was nothing left in me. When I got up and washed my face, I asked God what he wanted me to do. He told me to meditate on what it would be like if my husband came home and told me he had been unfaithful. He told me to imagine what pain my children would go through if this actually happened. Grief and pain is all I could feel. After about a week of sorrow and grief, he told me to now imagine what it would be like if I had been unfaithful and had to tell my husband and children. Imagine the pain and devastation adultery could cause.

For about three weeks, I was sick to my stomach and found it difficult to eat. I can remember the Lord telling me to eat something. I do not know how long I actually went without eating, I just remember feeling pain, sorrow, grief, shame, and humility. When I asked God why I could not eat, he told me this is what it means to fast. The true fast is when you are so broken you are not able to eat.

*"Remember when I was asked why my disciples and I did not fast? I answered when the groom is with the friends they have no need to fast, but when the groom is taken from the friends, then they shall mourn."*

Then came to him the disciples of John, saying, Why do we and the Pharisees fast oft, but thy disciples fast not?

And Jesus said unto them:

Can the children of the bridechamber mourn, as long as the bridegroom is with them? but the days will come, when the bridegroom shall be taken from them, and then shall they fast.

Matthew 9:14-15

"Lord, are you telling me fasting and mourning are the same?"

*"Yes. Fasting is just a way to teach you about grief and mourning."*

"Is it wrong to fast like in church?"

*"No, it is just a shadow of the real."*

"So being this sorrowful is not bad?"

*"No."*

"Then what is the difference between this and depression?"

*"The difference is my guidance. I told you to eat of my broken body and drink my blood in remembrance of me. If you did it unworthily, you would be weak, sick or sleep (die). To drink unworthily is in self-pity, not true understanding. Proverbs tells you, 'with all you're getting, get understanding. If it cost you all that you have . . . get understanding.'" To understand is the same as to know."*

Wisdom is the principal thing; therefore get wisdom: and with all thy getting get understanding.

Proverbs 4:7

Understand = (attend, consider, be cunning, diligent, direct, discern, eloquent, feel, inform, instruct, have intelligence, know, look well to, mark, perceive, be prudent, regard, skill (-ful), teach, think; (cause, make to, get, give, have) understand (-ing)

*"This word 'know' is a very intimate word. It is the same word used in Genesis, "Adam <u>knew</u> Eve and bore a son." There are many different levels of words. Your understanding has been limited. I am going to teach you to see with My eyes. Your eyes are blinded, but that is okay, don't worry, it too has its purpose. You can <u>know</u> someone physically and/or intimately. I am talking about heart intimacy (to <u>know</u> me) not sexual intimacy. The way Adam <u>knew</u> Eve is a type of heart intimacy.*

*This word 'know' can mean both. Sexual intimacy is only an outward expression to teach you about true intimacy of the heart (spirit). You may find it hard to compare the two, because your perception is twisted. In time you will understand and it will be clear. Hearing it for the first time may be uncomfortable. That is because people have used sex as a means to fulfill a void. In many ways people have perverted the purpose of sex.*

*Sex cannot fill your spirit. Sex is a gift to teach you about true intimacy; as well as to give you the gift of physical pleasure and parenthood. Just as a child is conceived through sexual intercourse, my word is conceived in knowing me through your emotions in your heart. The gift of children can open your eyes as to what love is and what love is not.*

*When a man's seed is implanted in the womb, life is the outcome. Not by the work of man's hands, but by the miracle of life. When people are intimate with Me, by knowing Me and My creation, My words become life and truth to them, by and through their emotions. What you experience in the physical teaches you about the spiritual (unseen) part of life.*

*Many people who claim to know Me are blind and have no clue who they are, much less who I am. Like Helen Keller, they need a teacher who can show them through their senses how to hear, see and speak. Your emotions work just like your five senses. I have taught you this.*

*Everything that is created is speaking. You have been taught sound and light are different dimensions of the same thing. It is the length of the waves, which determine whether you can see or hear them.*

*If the sun is speaking to you and you have never heard it, how much louder a light would you need to hear? Can you think of anything louder or brighter than the sun?*

*Understand? You are truly blind and deaf. You only think you have been able to see and understand. You believe what you have been taught by others and what life has taught you. Apart from Me it is impossible for you to see clearly. It is time for you to learn from Me. I will teach you to see with My eyes and to hear with My ears."*

You see, to acquire true understanding it is going to cost you. Example: Have you ever lost a loved one to death; your mother, father, spouse, or a child? If your answer is no, then you cannot understand the pain of those who have suffered such a loss.

We can imagine it, but we do not actually understand. The only way for one to understand (to know) the heart is one to have the same loss. One day, if I do not precede my loved ones in death I too, shall understand this painful truth.

Long ago a man named King Solomon prayed for an understanding heart. Because of this unselfish prayer God gave him wisdom greater than any man had ever been given. I was taught my whole life he prayed for wisdom. Isn't it weird how we believe what we have been taught opposed to looking it up for ourselves or asking God?

Feeling is understanding, and understanding is knowing. How can I know or understand others if I do not know or understand myself? This is what God was showing me.

The problem is I have not liked myself and have spent most of my life trying to change others and myself. Can we change the color of our skin or can a leopard change his spots? If I cannot change myself, how am I supposed to become a better person?

The reality of my inability to change myself sickened me. Feelings of hopelessness seemed to swallow me whole. Ironically, my acceptance of the fact, I cannot change myself, was the beginning of my transformation.

I was taught we all need to change ourselves. Prior to this experience with God, I agreed and taught this concept also. However, I now realize I cannot change myself, much less change another person.

In teaching this newfound truth you would not believe the opposition I have had to endure. Many have argued with heated words, and sometimes I used harsh language to make my point. I did not mean to offend with my argument, but I was desperately seeking a way to open their eyes.

Someone would typically challenge me with the argument: "We can change and we must take responsibility for our change."

I would respond with something like this: "Okay. Then why don't you decide to just loose the weight you are responsible for and get down to a healthy weight? If you have the power to do so, then why haven't you done so?" The argument usually just stops there. I am not so sure they actually believe they cannot change themselves, but it does stop the argument and makes them think about their inability to change at will.

You see if we could change, we would. If I can help others to see this, then change has begun in our minds. The first change must take place on the inside. Truth will change us. Without truth there is no change, and the truth I was faced with was I am hopelessly and utterly helpless.

Through judging the prostitute and others, and then becoming or doing the same thing or worse, I have realized we are all the same. Judgment has become a gift, which brings true humility.

I also thought my will was free and that too was an illusion. The apostle Paul put it this way, "The things I want to do, I do not. And the things I do not want to do, I do. Who will deliver me from this body of death?"

Jesus told us we could do nothing without him and our best is as filthy rags. So what do we do now? Remember, I was thankful I was not like the whore only to discover I was worse off than the whore. At least she could see herself. I was a blind hypocrite. I claimed to love God and was a spiritual whore.

We will continue to see judgment is a gift like no other.

# *Journal*

---

---

---

---

---

---

---

---

---

---

---

# Chapter 6

## The Promise.
## "If I cannot be good, then what?"

Back in the days of Moses, the people wanted rules and a king. They wanted someone else to talk to God on their behalf. However, God wanted to lead them by their hearts.

The people were stubborn and kept asking for a king, so God gave them what they asked for. The Law.

The Ten Commandments.

However, he warned they could not be kept. He did promise however, there was coming a day he would take out their hearts of stone and give them a heart filled with the spirit of God; He promised in that day they "shall walk in God's statutes and keep his commandments." It was the promise of God that would change the people not their own strength or attempt to follow the law.

So even unto this day people all over the world are still trying to keep God's commandments and be good. I now understand some of what God was telling me. I had tried all of my life to be good. I was now on a journey of becoming aware of just how twisted my thoughts actually were and still are.

Upon observing my condition and the condition of mankind, I realized we are like the darkness of the night sky and God alone is the light that shines in the darkness. Upon looking at myself, I feel like the chief of all sinners. Which sin is worse, mine which is to doubt God and believe a lie (Satan being the father of that lie), or the woman who whores to survive? The physical is temporary, but the spirit is eternal.

Living in this human body and not knowing my spiritual self is like being in the presence of God and not knowing He exists. Knowing oneself is much harder than it sounds. I call it brutal truth. It is much easier to lie to myself than to accept the truth.

I convinced myself I believe God loves me, yet to worry about anything is clear evidence I only *want* to believe he loves me. You see, if we love our children and are able to feed them, would we let them starve? Of course not. So when I see people starve in the earth, I ask God why, and this makes me question his love. I do not like this truth about my judgments of God, but the truth cannot be denied.

So what am I trying to say? Ultimately, I have realized I am not good. I cannot keep God's commandments and even if I want to make good choices, I am very limited to what I can and cannot do. Basically, I am broken and powerless.

<u>God promised us if we came to him with a broken and contrite heart he would heal us and give us a new heart.</u> In my attempt to become good through human efforts I was trying to fulfill *His* promise to give us a new heart. How did I equate being good with a new heart. I guess I assumed if I changed myself from evil to good, this would be success. I now understand I cannot fill His shoes. So I have to accept myself as I am. Think about it. If we could keep the commandments, why would we need God to give us a new heart by way of a promise? God's desire is a tenderhearted relationship built on love, while man wants rules to follow.

This was a major problem for my way of living. When you spend your whole life trying to be good, and to escape all the pain in your heart, somehow you believe you have accomplished it. Until you hit your own rock bottom of truth . . . I did not have control, nor could I attain it.

*"Now we are getting somewhere,"* God told me. *"Only after you realize you are blind, deaf, broken, and unable, can we begin the journey to the promise. To recognize you must surrender, is the same as when the seed burst in the ground and surrenders to the heat and pressure."*

How many times have you looked for the steps to success? This kind of thinking is evidence that the ten steps God gave us are somehow not enough. The problem is, the commandments were never given to us to keep. They were given to us to show us we cannot keep them. So what do we do after we discover we can do nothing?

Jesus prayed we would be one with Him and His Father as well as one with one another. It is about relationship. Knowing our own self, knowing mankind, and knowing God. Only then can we love ourselves, our neighbors, and God.

*"Is it possible to know another person if you do not know yourself?"*

*"No."*

*"Is it possible to love others if you do not love yourself?"*

*"No."*

*"Is it possible to love yourself if you do not accept all of you; if you pretend you are something or someone other than the true you? No is the only answer. Without the truth, you are only loving an image of yourself and others; another lie."*

What mask are you wearing so you will like yourself?

What mask do you wear so others will accept you?

Are you ready to face the true you? Can you look at yourself and see the truth about your nature?

Here is a look at the real me. I do not like it, but it is the brutal truth. I can be nice, polite, cordial, hospitable, and kind; as long as you meet up to my expectations. However, if you violate me, or my family, then the real me will come out from behind the mask and defend my loved ones. If you hurt my children or if I perceive you will, I quickly find my ability to hate and even murder. If you mess with my husband, I will quickly defend myself. So my true nature is hate, revenge, justice, survival, and even murder. I wish this was not the truth, but I must face it to deal with it.

You should hear just how rude I can be when I am in traffic and by myself. Sometimes I embarrass myself when I am the only one in the car. I am ashamed after I let all kinds of four letter words fly. I wish I never acted like this, but the truth is I do.

The truth be known, you are probably just like me. Whether or not you want to admit it is another story. Or maybe you have persuaded yourself you have changed, and you are no longer like this.

I have had some people argue the point that they could hate no one. My response is let someone murder your child and lets see if that changes. Hate is in us all. Some of us just hide it better than others. I am not saying we all act on our thoughts, but I am saying we all have them. We carry this sinful nature from birth.

I hid my hatred and even convinced myself: because I love God I do not hate anyone. However, one day while sitting with my husband and watching TV, I was disgusted with the hate and criticisms coming out of my husband's mouth. I prayed within myself, "God, how can I love someone who is so filled with hate?"

*"I will show you,"* was his response.

"Oh, no!" I thought to myself. I knew I had just judged myself as better than my husband because I could not see myself so filled with hate. This is what it means to think more highly of myself than others.

Less than one week from this prayer, I was on the phone with my parents and I overheard one of my sisters say something about me which was very mean and hypocritical. I overheard everyone in the room laugh at me. I was furious. You see she was mocking me about something that had happened over 10 years ago, of which she said she had forgiven me for.

Instead, she had actually mocked me for 10 years and pretended to be my friend. She even had other family members in on her revenge and no one protected me.

I was so angry I began to shake. All of the mean things she had done our whole life began to flood my heart and mind. Hatred like I could not imagine filled my body and spirit. I actually wanted to murder her. I could not believe my own thoughts. I began to wonder, if I could murder her and not get caught. If that were possible that is what I wanted to do to relieve myself of this pain. However, I struggled within myself, how could I claim to teach about God and his love if I could hate so much?

Amazingly my prayers were something like, "God, if I could kill her without You knowing it, I would." My hatred was so intense my bones actually began to hurt.

Thoughts of forgiveness plagued me. The Bible says, "If I say I love God who I can't see, but hate someone I can see, then I am a liar and the truth is not in me."

I later called her and cussed her for everything she had done to me in my life. I told her how bad I hated her and reminded her of what a horrible person she was. We talked for hours, doing nothing but fighting. Her response to me was I just needed to "get over it" and "grow up" and "stop wearing your feelings on your shoulders." Finally, at two o'clock in the morning, I hung up the phone. It was obvious she would never apologize for anything she had ever done. Hatred engulfed me. My attempts to forgive were utterly fruitless.

I was faced with the horrible notion maybe I did not love God. Scripture was testifying against me. I cried everyday for three weeks begging God to help me forgive her. I was desperate in my cries.

It was so bad I actually went to the hospital fearing I was having a heart attack.

When I asked God why he would not help me to forgive her, he responded, *"This is how you love someone who is so filled with hate, my child. I still love you and I loved you knowing you would do this. I loved you before and I will never stop loving you, no matter what you ever do."*

The memory of me asking God how I could love my husband when he was so filled with hate came rushing into my mind. Oh, God, I am so sorry for thinking I was better than my husband. Please forgive me. I have discovered I am not able to forgive as an act of my will. Will you do it for me, God?

I came to the conclusion my definition of love was not accurate. God loved me in spite of myself and I loved others if they measured up to my expectations and my standard of morality. I was taught forgiveness is a choice, but no matter how much I desired to forgive, the hatred and unforgiveness remained.

I had to face the truth, forgiveness was not a choice. It was something much greater than that. Only God could deliver me now.

That night the phone rang and it was my sister on the phone. She was weeping so hard it was difficult for her to speak. Through no effort of my own, forgiveness flooded my heart. I was so surprised at how it was suddenly there with no effort and she had not even apologized.

She could hardly speak. I began to cry and tell her I loved her and I was sorry for hating her.

She found her voice and asked me to forgive her. She told me she was struggling with forgiving someone in her life, as if she was aware of my own personal struggles. She was stuck, because the person would not admit to their betrayal. She told me how God kept telling her to "just get over it," "grow up," "don't wear your feeling on your shoulders." "Just follow your advice you gave your sister."

She continued, "All I could hear was the words I kept telling you and how impossible it was to do. God showed me our feelings and how we make each other feel is the basis of all relationships. I am so sorry. I had no idea how I made you feel, until it happened to me."

We talked for a while and my heart was broken to see how her judgments of me came back on her too. Here it was again. Judgment was something I thought I could stop doing because it was bad. I had persuaded myself I did not judge people, just their sin. What a joke. I judge all the time. I was learning judgment has a way of making us see ourselves and bringing us into humility. Judgment makes us all equal.

After we hung up the phone, I asked God what had just happened. How is it by just hearing her cry, forgiveness flooded me. I did not know she was going to apologize. For all I knew, she could have been calling to give me some bad news about our family. Just the sound of her voice hurting caused compassion to rise up in me. Why?

God responded: *"without the shedding of blood, there is no forgiveness."*

"I do not understand. I thought that was talking about Jesus dying on the cross for my sins."

*"Yes, that is true too. However, that was the physical blood atonement. The physical reveals the spiritual. Your spiritual blood is what pumps through your spiritual heart. Your spiritual blood is your feelings.*

*At the shedding of her emotions and tears, forgiveness was born. The reason humans do not forgive is usually because no sorrowful emotions are expressed. No blood is shed. If someone hurts you and is truly sorrowful and you can see or hear it in their face and voice; forgiveness is instant. However, if someone apologizes and there are no genuine emotions to accompany it, you are stuck in un-forgiveness. This is what Jesus was showing you by offering up himself as a blood sacrifice."*

"God, is there anyway I could have forgiven her without her having to suffer the same thing she judged me for?"

*"Yes. That is the way of the cross. I so loved you and my creations I sent my son before you ever asked for forgiveness, and before you were truly sorrowful for what you had done.*

*This way is not possible in the physical mind, accompanied by some set of steps. It is only possible when <u>We</u> are one in your spirit. You cannot do it alone."*

"How then can I do it? I prayed and asked for your help. Why didn't you help me when I prayed?"

*"It was not possible for you to understand or even desire this way until you saw the way of judgment.*

*However, now that you are beginning to understand the way of judgment and you have asked for another way, it will be given to you. It is the way of love. It is the way of the promise. This will take time, but through understanding the nature of mankind, compassion will began to grow in you. When compassion matures in you like fruit on the vine, you will experience forgiveness by way of love and understanding.*

*This is not an action you can decide to do and then act on it. It is a way of living. It is a gift that will be born out of a relationship with me. This way is the way of understanding in your spirit not your head. When you felt her pain in your heart, you desired a better way. Remember, <u>in the mourning you wake up</u>.*

*You cannot walk with me out of a decision alone. It is by walking without me and realizing you are not able to accomplish what you deem to be good, when you give up and come to the realization: you need me. As long as you thought you could forgive on your own, you would not ask for my help. However, when the hatred in you was so big you could not escape or muster up forgiveness, you called on me and asked for help."*

"God I am so sorry! Please forgive me."

*"I already have. It's okay. I know you and your nature. I am not offended at your nature; I made you and know you.*

*I rejoice to see you grow and discover the way of love. That is why you came to earth. You are learning living independent from me and trying to please me by keeping a set of rules is not the way. Relationship is not based on a set of rules. Relationship is nurtured out of intimacy. This takes time and I am not in any hurry. I am time.*

**"Thank you Father, I love you."**

*"I love you too."*

**"Without rules for me to live by, how will I know how to serve you?"**

*"It is not about serving me out of a set of rules. It is about loving each other and doing what you do out of the motivation of love. This is the promise of the new heart as a gift and not the law out of right and wrong."*

# Journal

# *Chapter 7*
## *Judge and see yourself.*

*"Scientifically, what are you made of?"*

**"What do you mean Lord?"**

*"Your body, what is it most made of?"*

**"Are you talking about water? We are mostly made of water, about 87% I think, if my memory serves me."**

*"Yes, exactly. You have said people who claim to know me and are 'born again' are now alive and other people are dead in their sin."*

**"Yes, I have been taught this and I believe it is what the Bible teaches."**

*"What do you see if you look at a dead body of water?"*

"My reflection I guess."

*"Correct answer, your very own reflection. Therefore, if the self proclaimed living church looks out at other people and sees their sins, whose sin are they actually seeing?"*

"Based on the dead water we just talked about, I would have to say the Church's own reflection. It would be the Church's sin."

*"Again you have answered well. You're looking into a mirror and seeing yourself. When you judge another person, that same judgment will be judged back unto you.*

"Lord I am sorry, I don't want to do that any more. I am learning every time I judge another person I turn into them."

*"No my child, you are not turning into them, you are already like them. All of mankind is broken. I did not come to condemn you, you are condemned already. Mankind is in a fallen nature. Remember, if you have broken one law you have broken them all. You are just blind to this truth. My Holy Spirit came to teach you about righteousness, judgment and sin."*

"Yes Lord, I have learned about these three in the Bible."

*"Are you saying you already know what they are?"*

"Yes God, I know you have made me righteous through Jesus and I know sin is wrong, and I know not to judge others."

*"Oh. Then My Holy Spirit must not know you already know this, for that is why he came. Maybe he forgot you already knew."*

This caught me off guard. I did not consider I was being presumptuous. But this question caused me to see my own arrogance; I wonder if he spoke this way to get my attention. One thing is for sure; it made it easy to distinguish His voice from mine.

"Oh, God I am sorry. I was taught in church what righteousness, judgment, and sin mean. Are you telling me we do not really know the truth about them?"

*"Yes, my dear, I am teaching you that you lack understanding and My precious Holy Spirit desires to teach you this truth and all truth."*

"Please God teach me about these truths."

"We have already begun. You have seen how you and the harlot on the television show are one. If I were to ask you how you discovered this great truth about yourself and I wanted to reward your teacher, who would you say showed you this wisdom."

"I would have to say the harlot I saw on the television show. I would have to say, please give her the reward, for without her suffering and her tragic story, I would not have seen my own sin of harlotry."

"You would have answered well. She was sent to you as a gift to open your eyes and great will be her reward. This is the mystery of Judgment. You have been taught judgment is bad and you should not do it.

*Therefore, you have tried for a long time to stop this action. However, when Adam and Eve ate from the tree of the knowledge of good and evil, it was passed down to all mankind. Judgment is in you. You cannot stop. However, you can understand and return to Me, "The Tree of Life." When you see yourself as one with others, by way of judgment, you will see the condition of mankind and why Jesus had to die. You will be given the gift of understanding and compassion.*

*Without judgment you will deem yourself righteous by your deeds. Or you will say you are righteous by the way of forgiveness, yet you cannot choose to forgive, it is a gift. Many of today's leaders teach people that it is right and good to forgive; and will even go so far as to teach unless you forgive you cannot be forgiven. However, they lack understanding. They themselves teach others to do what they cannot.*

*You too believed this and taught it until you learned with your sister you could not forgive no matter how much you desired to. It was a gift. It always comes as a gift."*

"Why is it then, I could forgive other things, which did not seem so bad?"

*"This is because you had already received forgiveness for the same deeds. Understand, when you have recognized your sin and another person sins the same sin against you, forgiveness for that sin is already in you and therefore you have it to give away. However, if someone commits a sin you think you are not capable of doing, you have not received forgiveness for that sin, and therefore forgiveness for that is not in you. How can you give something away you have not yet received for yourself?*

*Remember how you thought you were different from the harlot? But then you became aware you also suffered the same sin condition? Likewise, you have all manner of sin in you, you are just not aware of them all. Sinful is the condition of mankind. It is love that heals you. Note it was not until you saw how deep your sin is that you could begin to see how deep my love is. Seeing your darkness gives you the ability to see Light (Me). Remember the midnight sky."*

I was reminded of a story when a very dear friend of mine came to me one day, heartbroken and crushed. This person had been in church for five years and had done all she knew to serve and know God. She had followed every rule given to her by the Church leaders and she had received Jesus' sacrifice as atonement for her sin.

Through her flood of tears and groaning she told me she had just discovered her husband was having an affair. She began to curse her mistress calling her a drug addict, whore, bitch and a home wrecker. She vowed how she could never be or do anything like this and asked me how God could allow this to happen to her.

I had been teaching her about judgment and understanding. I told her I would help her and we could ask God to give us understanding so she would not have to walk this same path. I ask her to consider where in her life she could have this same sin. Maybe it could be a spiritual sin like I discussed earlier (Spiritual harlotry). She was appalled at the suggestion that she could do such a thing; after all she loved God and therefore could not commit such a sin.

My heart sank and I prayed in my mind. "Lord, please tell me what to do."

*"Love her when she returns."*

"What! What about restoring a brother and what about helping her through this?"

*"Which would you prefer: for her to stand before me with unforgiveness for her mistress, and to have never committed physical adultery. Or for her to receive understanding and to stand before me a mistress forgiven for her sin, with forgiveness in her heart for her own mistress?"*

"The latter, Lord. I know if she does not forgive, then she cannot be forgiven. Please have mercy on her Lord."

*"This is my mercy. I love her more than anything she can do. I am not afraid of her walking out her judgment so she can receive and give forgiveness."*

About three months later my friend came to my house and wanted to tell me something. God spoke in my heart and told me she was doing everything she had judged her mistress for and now was the time to show her His love. Before she could speak, I asked her if I could say what she was about to tell me.

"What do you mean?" She replied.

I then repeated to her every accusation she had against her mistress, and told her God still loved her.

She fell on the floor and began to weep and yell. "Oh, my God! Please forgive me, I am just like her. I now understand, help me. Please deliver me; I am the bitch, I am a drug addict, I am the whore. Oh God, I am everything I said I would not be. I am just like her. Please forgive us both."

She began to weep and cry for the lady who had destroyed her family. Because she had received forgiveness for herself, she now had forgiveness to give away. God's love so filled and forgave her, I witnessed forgiveness coming out of her uncontrollably. God did through her what she could not do herself.

I asked God if there was another way. Why did she have to learn by experience? I was so sorrowful not only for her but for the entire human race. We are all dammed to this judgment and then becoming what we judge.

*"It is not as you see it. This is not the only way. Sometimes however, you must taste the hot pepper before you will believe it is hot, because it remains cold to the touch. Many times there is more to life than what meets the eye.*

*So you see, sometimes experience is the only teacher you will accept. However, after you have been burned by your independence, you are less likely to go it on your own. Judgment is not the culprit, your perception is. Judgment is actually the vehicle by which you shall receive humility. I give grace to the humble, and I resist the proud."*

I am often reminded of judgment and my nature. I was going down the road one day and came to a four-way stop intersection. The other person ran through the stop sign and I began to shout out loud in my car. "How stupid can you be? Are you blind? You idiot! You may not care about your life, but what about mine?" Suddenly, I heard, *"I will show you how easy it is to be so stupid."*

"Oh, God I am sorry, have mercy on us."

I kid you not, before I reached the next stop sign, a for sale sign caught my attention and I was reading the phone number trying to memorize it so I could call and check on this house, when all of a sudden I realized I was running a four-way stop sign. I slammed on my breaks before I entered the middle of the intersection and shouted, "Oh God!"

*"See, that is how you could be so stupid."*

I began to kind of laugh and cry at the same time. The realization of humanity seemed to be upon me. Without mercy and grace we are all damned. God is our only hope. Love is our only hope. Inside each and every one of us is judgment and damnation.

If I wrote all of my judgment stories, I would have to write multiple volumes.

Beware, I have taught this for years and many people argue with me and say they do not judge others or that, "I would never be like so and so, God has changed me . . ." Only to discover they too are not exempt from this law of judgment. Like gravity we are all touched by it. The Spirit of God, Our Creator, The Master of the Universe; no matter what you call him, he is here to teach us all about judgment.

I talk a lot about judgment, only because it is such a great teacher. Many of the truths I have discovered have come to me through judgment.

I no longer try to stop judging, but rather I look for God's hand and listen for His voice to teach me more. Judgment is a gift of love from God, which clothes us all in humility. What greater gift could we ask for than humility? Remember, God gives grace to the humble.

# Journal

_____

_____

_____

_____

_____

_____

_____

_____

_____

_____

_____

# Chapter 8
## Why didn't they tell me? They lied to me!

When I began to discover these truths, I became very angry at the church and the church leaders. I tried to talk to my leaders and tell them what I had heard from God. However, no one seemed to understand my frustration or what I was talking about.

When God asked me why I was mad, I told Him I felt lied to.

*"You can only teach what you know, and you hear what you are able. I make the eyes to see and the ears to hear. I also make the blind and the deaf. Do you want to blame me?"*

"No, of course not; but I would like to find someone to blame."

*"Just like Adam and Eve, yet again. When your son asked you where babies come from did you lie to him?"*

"No."

*"What did you tell him?"*

"I told him, God gave Daddy a seed and he put it in Mommy's tummy, and God made it grow and then the baby comes out of Mommy's tummy."

*"Tell me the story you told him when he got older."*

"God you know."

*"I know that I know, but humor me anyway."*

First, I need to tell you what he said when he came home from a wildlife safari. My son went to the Global Wildlife Center near our home, and while there he witnessed the birth of a giraffe. The second he walked in the door, he said "Mama! You better be glad you are not a giraffe." I said, "I am very glad I am not a giraffe, but tell me why I should be so glad."

"I just saw a baby giraffe be born, and you should see where they come from. They come right out of the mama's butt, and then they fall six feet to the ground!"

"Wow! Son, I am really glad I am not a giraffe!"

A few years later he asked me how Daddy put the baby seed in my tummy and where did Daddy keep these seeds God gave him.

As you can imagine I struggled with this question and how to answer it. So I asked him if he remembered when he told me I should be really glad I was not a giraffe, because they come out of the mama's butt. He said, "Yes."

"Well," I said, "he did not come out of her butt." He began to tell the whole story again to assure me it did indeed come out of her butt. So, I explained to him about the anatomy of a woman.

"Remember when your baby sister was born and you wanted to know why she did not have a te-te, like you?"

"Yes."

"Well that is because God made boys and girls different and we do not have the same kind of te-te."

"What kind do you have?" He asked.

"Girls have a vagina. It is on the inside of our bodies not on the outside like boys. It is very close to the butt; however it is not the butt. That is why it looked like the giraffe was coming out of the butt. It was actually coming out of the vagina. That is were babies come from."

"I did not come from there! I came from a seed that Daddy got from God. You told me so. You lied to me, you lied! You said I came from a seed out of your tummy."

"Daddy did get the seed from God, and he did put it in my tummy. You just never asked me how? So I never told you about the male anatomy and how the seed was put in my tummy but now that you are a big boy and you are asking me I am telling you how."

So I told him the rest of the story about men and women and where babies come from. Afterwards he asked me, "Are you and Daddy going to have any more babies?"

"No." I replied.

"Good! Then you never have to do that again!"

As you can imagine; I did not tell him anything else about sex nor did I tell him it was not the last time his dad and I would ever do that.

*"So why didn't you tell him how the seed got into the mommy's tummy when he first asked you where babies came from?"*

"He was not ready for that much truth yet."

*"Oh, so you do understand why I did not reveal this truth to you earlier."*

"God, are you telling me I was not ready? How do I know when others are ready and who to share this with?"

*"It is not about you being ready as much as it is about the timing being right. There is a time for everything. I decide when and where and by whom I plant my fields.*

*My words are my seeds and man's heart is my field. Is it wise for you to blame my farmers for planting my seed, but not showing you their fruit? Can a farmer make fruit or do I?*

*Do you still need someone to blame? If so, blame me. If not simply share this truth and trust me to bring the understanding to the hearts that are open to these words."*

"God, I am sorry, I did not understand. I just felt so cheated. I worked so hard to know you and to understand your word. All I wanted was to please you. I trusted them to teach me."

*"Exactly, you trusted people to teach you instead of trusting me to teach you. Understand, many generations have prayed and sought to know me and my word. In time, all of my creation will know me and my word.*

*I am teaching you this language, a language of symbols. I am opening your eyes to truth which is hidden in creation.*

*Jesus taught in parables, and I am teaching you the same way. You will share this with others and help others to see what you are seeing.*

*When you teach this language to others, remember, truth comes in levels. It starts out as a seed and then it grows into something much greater than itself. If you show a child an acorn and tell him a giant oak tree is inside of the acorn, he would not be able to comprehend this truth. He may even think you are teasing or lying to him. However, in time he will come to understand a giant oak was truly inside of the acorn.*

*My word and truth are like this. Some people will not understand. Some will actually think you are lying or are actually deceived. However, in time, truth will reveal itself and all shall understand the fruit and the majestic trees of my word."*

*Journal*

# Chapter 9

## The Necessity of Positive and Negative.

I am by no means a scientist, nor do I have any formal education other than the basics in high school. This is not a lesson in science, but rather a look at the atom in order to reveal the fact that both positive and negative are necessary for life. By definition, atoms have no overall electrical charge. This means there must be a balance between the positively charged protons and the negatively charged electrons. Atoms must have an equal number of protons and electrons. For example, an atom of krypton must contain 36 electrons since it contains 36 protons.

Remember this is not a lesson on atoms, and I am not even going to discuss ions; I am only using the atom to show you about the necessity of negative and positive energy. Going any further would take us off track and we would loose our focus. Note, however, if we take the atom and study it in great detail, we could learn an immeasurable amount of wisdom concerning our emotions.

I have heard others talk about ridding themselves of something they call "negative energy." All I know about this concept is what I have heard others mention on television, and what I have read about it in a couple of books. All speakers seem to have the common stance: getting rid of negative energy is helpful. However, even the basics of all life show us negative energy is necessary for anything to exist. This is the creation showing us truth yet again.

I needed to find some way, to show others how painful emotions, sometimes called negative energy by others; is not avoidable, but rather is necessary in our lives.

Everything in the universe is held together by a positive and negative charge. Take two magnets for example and put the two positive ends together. It is impossible. Put the two negative ends together. This too is impossible. They will repel each other. Both are needed for union. Atoms are in a continual state of searching for balance, by either acquiring or surrendering electrical charges.

In order for a current of energy to flow, both positive and negative must engage to create power. Therefore, both positive and negative are necessary for power to exist and move. If you could somehow remove all of the negative energy in the world, it would cease to exist. It is simply not possible.

This part of creation is telling us removing the negative energy from our lives is an illusion. You may have found a measure of strength to exercise self-control and think on good thoughts, but that action does not make the pain actually go away. When we attempt to rid ourselves of pain, it finds another way to manifest in our lives.

Medical professionals agree stress causes disease and illness. Attempting to rid our lives of negative energy is actually a form of ignoring or redirecting it. Matter can neither be created nor destroyed; it can only change forms.

We have heard it said opposites attract. Male and female are terms used to describe electrical outlets, and the plug. A negative is necessary to receive the positive.

Remember earlier in the book I talked about asking for faith and doubt is given, for only in doubt is faith seen. Both positive and negative are absolutely necessary for: life, power, understanding, and sight.

It can be said without the negative, power cannot exist. If you understand this basic concept, you can know and rely on the fact, when a negative is present in your life, a positive is on its way. Power is on its way. Put your tongue on the end of a 9-volt battery, but only touch one of the terminals. You will feel nothing. However, put your tongue on both and you will experience the power.

Life is the same way. I no longer call my emotions good or bad. I no longer call them negative or positive. I call them pleasure or pain. I accept them both and seek God to help me receive the understanding they were sent to reveal. Together they somehow turn on the light of my perception and my understanding grows.

At this point I am reminded when I heard, *"Without darkness you cannot see."*

We must realize pain or darkness has a purpose. The fact the purpose is for our good brings about a peace, which can carry us through any pain life may bring our way.

*Journal*

_____

_____

_____

_____

_____

_____

_____

_____

_____

_____

_____

_____

# Chapter 10
## Feel the Feeling and Get the Understanding.

In the Book of Proverbs we are instructed to 'get understanding,' even if it costs us everything. Well, I am here to tell you feeling my feelings cost me my whole way of living and thinking. I am not the same person I was when I began this journey. Feeling my feelings has taught me my nature is pretty self-serving: I like justice for others, but mercy for me. I can be kind and generous as long as it doesn't cause me too much pain. I secretly want revenge, but want forgiveness afterwards.

Sometimes it appeared to be easier to stay in my delusions rather than face the truth; for many times the truth is brutal.

I had two paths set before me: stay with my defenses attempting to rid myself of every painful emotion which came my way; or be true to my heart and experience my emotions as they come to me with the gift of truth, understanding and humility.

First, I had to decide which road I wanted. To be honest, if I could have found a way to rid myself of my sorrows, I would have chosen that path. But I realized this path was a fruitless illusion, which only produced more and more suffering with no real changes in my life.

The latter however, has changed me from the inside out. After living most of my life on path number one, and turning in my most recent years to path number two, I never want to go back to the path of illusions. I will take the truth, pain and all, any day.

Living life true to my heart, and true to myself, is life. The other road is a path of survival.

Let me end by telling you one more story. This has changed my life so profoundly I share it every chance I get. Hang in there, don't give up and trust that you too can go through anything and be transformed into a truthful life. The You, you were meant to be.

I was sitting on my sofa one morning reading my Bible, when for no apparent reason I began to tremble violently. I physically was shaking out of control and a feeling of extreme fear overwhelmed me. This was weird because everything in my life at the time seemed so wonderful. I was happy and at peace. Nothing of any significance was going on. I stopped reading and prayed "Oh God, what is wrong with me?" No answer came back to me.

I looked down to read another scripture in hopes God would speak to me. Unbelievably I read these words, "Blessed is he who trembles in my presence."

I paused in disbelief, and questioned God; "Are you telling me I am trembling because I am in your presence right now?"

*"Yes"* Came the reply. *"Every time you have felt this type of feeling it was because you were experiencing my presence."*

"But this feels like fear."

*"And if you call it fear, then it is fear. Remember I told you, as a man thinks, so is he. However, if you believe my words and what I said, then you will have what you believe.*

*I did not give you a spirit of fear, but a spirit of power, love and a sound mind. If you call it fear, that is what you have, but if you call it the spirit of power, love and a sound mind, then that is what you have. Which one do you want?"*

"The spirit of power, love and a sound mind, of course. But, if it is you, then why does it feel so bad?"

*"I told you before, I am all power, and power can be painful and uncomfortable. However, like a piece of fine china, if you allow me to, I will temper your spirit and you will not feel so uncomfortable. This requires trust. Can you trust me in the midst of feeling pain?"*

"Yes, Lord, please help me trust you more."

As you can imagine this was mind-boggling and I questioned what I was hearing. However, just as he had said, in time, I became more comfortable with the trembling and the turning in my stomach. There were even times when things in my life, which should have produced the old familiar feelings of fear and anxiety, actually brought about in my heart feelings of unexpected peace.

When I questioned God as to why I was at so much unexpected peace, he told me it was because I was learning he loved me. The more I understand his love, the less fear and doubt enter my mind. Furthermore, whenever I had those feelings, I learned to call them the Spirit of Power and I relaxed into the trembling and turning feelings. I came to trust if the Spirit of Power was moving inside of me, whatever I was in need of, the Spirit of Power, was actually bringing it to pass. Sometimes my problems were actually solved before the trembling was over.

Now I don't fight the feelings or assume they are bad. I simply welcome the Spirit of Power, Love and A Sound mind . . . and wait to see what God is doing. One thing is for sure.

He is always loving me.

# Journal

# Chapter 11

## When I look at my shortcomings, all I can see is: He LOVES me.

Looking at my true self was not an experience of pleasure. Rather, I felt much pain, sorrow, grief, and guilt. How could anyone actually love me if they could see behind my mask and see the real me? God showed me how others could not love me until I learned to love myself.

I realized my attempt to be good was really an attempt to be loved by God and others; for I knew if they could ever see the real me, they would not love me. I deceived myself and others, but God is never deceived. He always sees the real me hidden inside, but loves me anyway.

This kind of love is impossible to me. But with God all things are possible. Remember God counted righteousness unto Abraham when he believed the impossible. I now know righteousness is accounted unto us when we see our true self and still believe God can and does love us. This is, believing the impossible. This is the opposite of self-righteousness. This is true righteousness.

Now facing my true self, I realize I am the midnight sky, and all the attributes of God, which shine out of me, are like the stars. I have no light of my own, but I am only a beautiful black backdrop for his love to be revealed. If ever, I think I can be good, then I am no longer in need of God. However, knowing my true self, allows me to surrender my thoughts, my feelings and my desires to the one true God of the universe; while I sit in awe of him that he would love me and choose to live in me and pour himself through me.

You too are loved, just as you are. Dark and lovely, the spirit of man is the lamp of God. So set your lamp on a hill and let God shine in you for others to behold: His LOVE.

For to whom much is forgiven, loveth much!

*Journal*

_____

_____

_____

_____

_____

_____

_____

_____

_____

_____

_____

# *Postscript*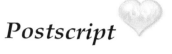

I hope I have sparked questions inside of you, which have not before been given the light of day in your thoughts. Even though we cannot change ourselves, truth absolutely changes us. As you allow yourself to think upon and seek for truth, change will come as a result of the truth you embrace.

As you can imagine I cannot return to my old way of thinking. I find myself looking back as though I am reading about another person entirely.

It was very difficult to keep each chapter concise and to the point, because I found myself getting off tract easily. I am currently working on lesson booklets to expound on various topics covered in this book. As a curtsey to you my reader, I intentionally did not do this when writing this book in order to tell my story.

There is so much to talk about it sometimes feels like a maze of knowledge. When I teach in a classroom setting, so many questions are sparked I am forced to rely on my flip chart and ask my participants to please stay with the lesson at hand. I would make a list of the questions and prepare lessons specifically for my students to teach at a later time. So please understand, I too had and will continue to have many questions. The answers I have found I share, while I continue working on those unanswered questions.

There is a whole world of creation filled with knowledge and wisdom. My dream is to give you the tools to hear and understand this language. Your emotions are necessary to perceive this language and getting to know and understand yourself is absolutely necessary for your journey.

I encourage you to take the time to heal your emotions and treat them as you would crippled legs that need to be rehabilitated in order to walk and run. In time you will find your emotions in a healed state are a gift to hear and perceive this language. I endeavor to share with you through print what I have discovered in this amazing language we call the universe.

# *About the Author*

Angela Q. Bertone has taught on the subject of the heart and spiritual matters since she was 19 years of age. Through the years her leaders have asked her to teach on many subjects and to people of all ages. As a businesswoman, she has earned the respect of her community and her colleagues.

She has also held healing retreats for broken women who suffered the loss of their children and or spouses. She counts these requests as an honor and has done this work as a volunteer.

Those who have studied her teachings have called her "A spiritual cardiologist." She is bold and often a blunt speaker who seeks for words to shock you into thinking: Hoping to get you out of the box. She takes joy in being a wife, mother, and grandmother. Angela retreats to the outdoors and has a passion for teaching on spiritual matters.

*Here are a few quotes from Angela's class participants:*

"Unique, entertaining and inspiring."

"She is an interesting in-depth conversationalist, with thought provoking responses. I could listen to her for hours."

"Your words were life altering for me because you helped me view my life through the eyes of God instead of my own eyes or the eyes of others. You brought me light years down the road toward healing my past hurts, feeling like a victim and blaming others for my circumstances. You got me un-stuck! (Not an eloquent description, but that is what you did for me!) Thanks for sharing your God-given gifts with me."

"She has the most amazing way of explaining a subject, that not only holds your interest, makes you desire more and more, helps you to understand things even the most difficult of people have a hard time teaching; but she also translates it in such a way you just KNOW she cares. She has a special gift."

"She is a life gate, a creative Spirit, a person of purpose. Heart-warming, captivating, charming and wise. She is a thought provoking and angelic-like being who challenges you intellectually and spiritually. She cares."

96368260R00126

Made in the USA
Columbia, SC
29 May 2018